Angelika Schmelzer

Moreton Morrell Site

Best
Turned Out!

Tips for a well groomed horse

Contents

Imprint

Copyright of original edition ©2003 by
Cadmos Verlag Brunsbek.
Copyright of this edition ©2003 by
Cadmos Equestrian, Brunsbek.
Translated by: Claire Williams
Editorial project management:
Editmaster Co., Northampton
Design and setting: Ravenstein, Verden.
Photographs: Angelika Schmelzer
All rights reserved
Copying or storage in electronic media is permitted
only with the prior permission of the publishers.
Printed in Belgium

ISBN 3-86127-938-X

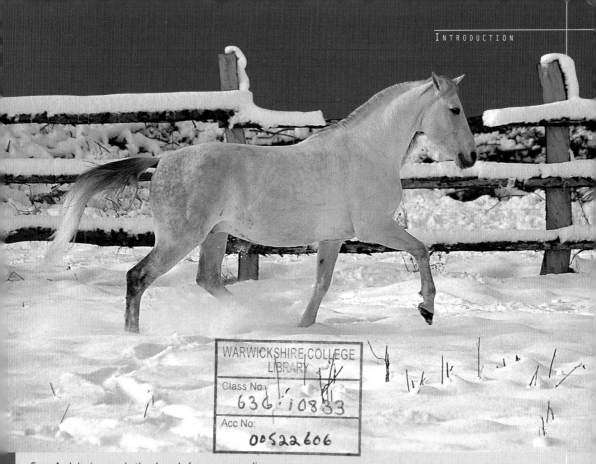

Even Andalusians and other breeds from warmer climes can cope well with winter conditions.

Introduction

Nature equips our horses and ponies with their own mini central-heating system: the skin, complete with a protective coat of body hair and longer hair such as mane and tail, fulfils a variety of important functions. Body heat is given off, cooling is achieved through the evaporation of sweat, warmth is conserved, rain is drained away and wind is kept out. As long as we humans don't interfere, then this protective system works so well that, for horses, there really is no such thing as bad weather. Most of the time they cope with the cold, wet, heat and storms much better than we do, and are happy to be outside whatever the weather.

First groom, then ride

Whenever we ride our horses, we inevitably interfere with Nature's grand plan, with grooming always taking place before any work. It is therefore vital that when grooming, we do it in such a way as to ensure that the natural protective functions of the skin and coat are interfered with as little as possible. We should avoid doing anything that might look good but that could result in harming our horse. We should always consider how our horses are kept, as this is an important factor. Horses kept outside all year round are considerably more reliant on the protection provided by their coats than those that are stabled.

The longer hair of the mane, forelock and tail acts as both a fly screen and rug.

Tips

To look after a horse properly, riders need to:

- understand the horse's natural protective mechanism of coat and hair
- keep this in mind when grooming so as to disrupt it as little as possible
- always keep in mind how the horse is kept.
  All ridden horses should be groomed daily, both before and after riding, as this serves more than one purpose:
- it helps the horse to wear its tack with out any sand or sweat residue causing skin irritations or saddle sores
- it strengthens the bond between horse and rider, as in the herd mutual grooming is an act of friendship
- it is an important contribution to the maintenance of a horse's general health, since the skin is its largest organ; and
- it lets you form an overall picture of your horse's condition (general wellbeing, condition, injuries, lumps and bumps

Horses kept outdoors are particularly reliant on their coats' protection.

Only squeaky clean horses make the best impression in the show ring.

The Full Wash

Before any competition, show or event, the coat, mane and tail should be thoroughly washed in order to remove any dirt, make dull hair shiny and facilitate the job of dressing the mane and tail.

Tips

When washing your horse, you should remember that:

- *it is really only possible in warmer weather, unless your yard has a horse solarium*
- *only specialist equine shampoo should be used, usually perfume - free and moisturising*
- *washing should only be done when absolutely necessary, at most every 4–6 weeks during warmer weather.*

Washing either too often or incorrectly can harm the horse since its coat's natural protection can be affec ted and the skin may suffer from irritation.

Quick Wash

It doesn't always have to be a full wash: especially at warmer times of the year, you can simply rinse your horse off after exercise with clean water, to get the sweat out of the coat. If left, dried sweat can be very itchy and attracts annoying insects. The legs can also be hosed or rinsed off with lukewarm water after training. As long as no shampoo is used, the protective mechanism of the skin and hair won't be impaired.

When rinsing, use a bucket of lukewarm water and a sponge, or a hose. Never use ice cold water, and if a hose is used, the stream of water should be not be too strong,

Tired legs will enjoy a gentle wash down.

Sweat should be washed out of the coat after work so that it doesn't cause irritation later.

otherwise you may startle or even hurt the horse. Avoid washing off hot or sweated up horses over the entire body immediately after exercise as, although this might be a good way of immediately cooling the horse down, it also results in a sudden decrease in circulation, meaning that metabolised waste products will not be removed from the horse's body as fast. A result of this can be bad muscle ache or even serious muscle strain.

Only after a thorough wash do white markings really look white, rather than yellowish.

rough cleaning may be beneficial in order to loosen and get rid of dandruff, scabs or the remains of creams or topical wound dressings

Tips

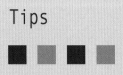

For a thorough wash you will require:

- *as much lukewarm water as possible, either from the hose or in buckets or watering cans*
- *shampoo suitable for horses*
- *a sponge or a dimpled rubber grooming mitt or curry comb*
- *a sweat scraper*
- *a rug of some type, ideally an old sheet or a large bath towel, in order to cover the horse while drying off*
- *somewhere to tie the horse up safely with good footing that won't get slippery when wet and that has good drainage.*

When hosing down always:
- begin at the bottom, starting with the legs, and work up over the shoulder, neck and chest
- avoid using a strong, cold stream of water
- avoid the loins and quarters.

Deep Clean

Before public appearances, the outer coat and all long hair should be thoroughly washed with shampoo to get rid of all dirt that may have collected over the months, leaving the coat dull or yellowish looking. Also during or after medical treatment a tho-

Working in twos is usually best, especially when having to deal with awkward buckets or watering cans.

First, thoroughly wet the whole coat, except for the horse's head. Apply shampoo sparingly to the sponge or grooming mitt, and then with circular movements and plenty of elbow grease, shampoo the entire horse. The mitt or curry comb can be used on the neck and torso, while the sponge can be used on sensitive or ticklish bits.

The coat, mane and tail are ideally washed all at the same time.

It is important to work quickly: washing the coat will leave it saturated down to the skin, and the horse will then get cold relatively quickly.

When rinsing, begin at the front and top and work backwards and down. Take care to rinse all the shampoo out of the coat.

Following this, use a sweat scraper to get excess water out of the coat, and finally rub the horse dry with an old towel. Until it is completely dry, either put the horse under a solarium, tie him up in a sunny sheltered spot covered with a light rug, or take him for a walk.

Wash, cut and comb

As part of the same process, but also separately, the mane and tail can be washed. First the forelock needs to be pulled back under the halter as far as possible so that your horse doesn't get any soapsuds in his eyes or on his face. In order to clean thoroughly long and often very dense tails, they should be really saturated – something that is often particularly difficult with ponies. Refer to pictures 1–4 on page 10. In the case of particularly dirty or stained tails this process may need to be repeated; otherwise, ring out the tail by hand and use a sweat scraper if necessary on the bits of the pony's body that may have become wet.

Never stand directly behind your horse when dealing with the tail; stand to one side.

Finally, it's off to a warm and sheltered spot for finger combing.

1. With a well-behaved horse, things are made easier by being able to dunk the tail into a bucket of luke-warm water. The mane is best dealt with by two people – one pours the water over, while the other massages it in.

2. Once the hair is wet enough the shampoo can be applied.

3. For both the mane and tail, the hair should be rubbed together using both hands. Especially in the case of the tail, ensure that the underneath and the depths of the thick tail are thoroughly shampooed since it's there that the most dirt accumulates.

4. Rinse off using a hose, watering can or bucket, ideally again in twos. This means that one person can pour the water as required, while the other massages the clean water in and ensures proper rinsing out of all the suds

The mane and tail need to be carefully looked after so they can fulfil their important tasks.

Splitting Hairs

The mane, tail and forelock are your horse-'s most beautiful natural feature, fulfilling at the same time the practical purposes of protection and warmth. When grooming, you need to therefore ensure that as few hairs are pulled out as possible – after all it takes years before a pulled tail hair reaches its full length again! It's for this reason that we don't roughly comb or brush out manes, forelocks and tails, and instead finger comb or "todder" the tail. Here's how.

Labour of love: finger combing

"Todder" or finger combing entails carefully separating each strand of hair one by one, without pulling any out. Knots are untangled; hairs that have fallen out are removed so that the entire length is tidy. After this test of patience the mane and tail will look full and free.

Before starting, the tail should be evenly shortened or banged (see page 13) and the end brushed through (see picture 1 on page 12), and then we can start.

1. First of all, with one hand grasp the tail a couple of hands-breadths up from the end, with the other hand brushing it through with a hairbrush.

2. Then lay the dock gently over your left arm or hold it with the left hand, while with the fingers of the right hand bit by bit grasp small strands of the tail and gently untangle and comb out the hair with your fingers so that it falls loosely to the right. Always only take as many strands as you can easily deal with, otherwise hairs may be pulled out or the horse may become unsettled.

3. In this way the entire tail can be combed out and it will be revealed in all its full glory.

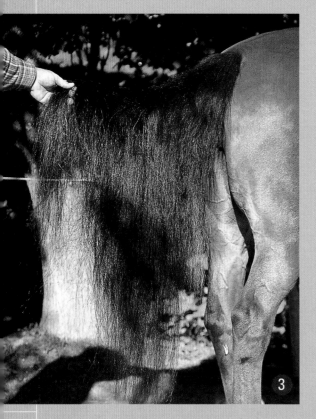

In order to shorten the tail (also called banging), lift it gently up and lay it over your forearm since, when moving, the tail doesn't hang straight down but instead is slightly lifted. With the other hand, grasp the tail and slide down to just above the required length. The end can then be trimmed across in a straight line with scissors.

The tails of competition and show horses are sometimes "pulled" by plucking out the hairs down both sides of the dock. This makes the tail look tidier and more elegant and may also help to improve the appearance of the hindquarters. It does, however, mean that rain can reach into the sensitive area around and under the top of the dock. For this reason many horse enthusiasts prefer not to pull their horses' tails.

To do the mane, a similar procedure is followed: to keep the part you are working on separate from the rest, turn the entire mane over to the opposite side of the neck. In the case of a thick mane that falls on both sides, or a short mane that won't lie over the neck, use a comb or clip to keep the mane in place. Beginning at the withers, start by separating out the mane with your fingers, strand by strand, and finally comb through the length carefully with a brush.

Shortening the Tail

It may be necessary to shorten the tail if it has grown so long that it touches the ground or the horse is constantly standing on it when getting up, in the process pulling out clumps of hair. Even a tangled or thin, frayed looking tail can be shortened, as this will help to make it look fuller. The tail should, at rest, reach no lower than the fetlock, but at least as far as the middle of the cannon bone.

Pulling a mane

A variety of traditions determine a horse's hairdo – in other words, whether the mane is shortened to a unified length or left "au naturel". In traditional competitive riding it is usual to shorten the mane to the length of a hand's breadth, by pulling or cutting.

In order that horses at grass or those kept outdoors year round are not deprived of the natural and necessary protection provided by manes and forelocks, these should be left long enough at least to cover the eyes and half of the neck. In summer this coverage wards off annoying insects, and in winter serves as insulation.

When manes are pulled regularly, the hairs that have grown longer than the required length are pulled out, thinning the mane. Before doing so, though, the horse should be worked, as this makes it easier to pull the hairs out. Begin at the poll and work down to the withers; where the mane should taper out horizontally. Pulling is a fairly unpleasant experience for most horses and some fight against it. In this case resorting to scissors is more horse friendly; and, with experience, achieves almost the same results, although the result may appear somewhat shaggier, since the mane is not thinned at the same time.

Another option for horses that resist mane pulling is the increasing range of devices that comb and cut the mane at the same time and result in a more natural look. These are widely available on the market.

1. First of all the mane should be thoroughly brushed or combed.

2. Then with a mane comb, comb the hair from the top to the required length. The remaining hair below is held, the rest pushed back to the top.

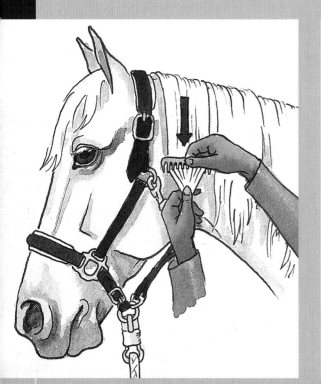

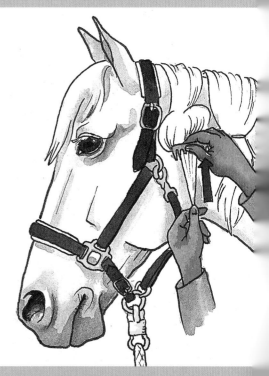

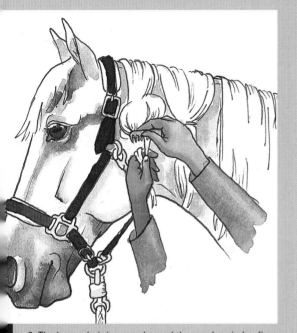

3. The longer hair is wound round the comb or index finger and ...

4.. ... pulled out with an energetic tug. The finished, shortened mane hairs are combed out and held back with a rubber band or hair clip so that they don't get in the way.

Cutting a bridle path

In Western riding in particular, it is usual for the mane behind the poll to be cut or clipped for up to 10 cm down the crest. The bridle path allows the headpiece to lie better and allows an easier view of the cheek on the side on which the mane falls. For horses with very thick manes, this allows the bridle to be put on easier, without the hassle of sorting out the forelock from the mane.

For many horses it is a fate worse than death to have someone fumbling behind their ears with scissors, or worse still clippers. The result can be a panic reaction, increasing the danger of injury on both

This profile looks more elegant, thanks to the clearly defined bridle path.

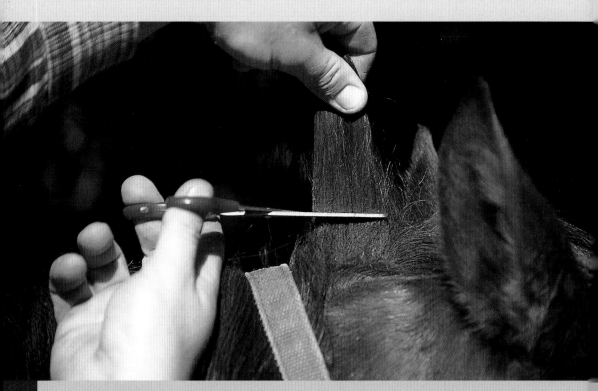

The mane should be cut short with scissors and then tidied up with clippers.

sides. It is therefore wise to use blunt-ended scissors, and to take plenty of time to get your horse used to the experience calmly.

First the forelock should be sectioned off and combed forward under the head collar. For horses with a sparse forelock, you can cheat a bit by simply combing more of the mane hairs forward from just behind the poll before you start cutting. The head collar should be pushed forward and the back edge of the bridle path marked. The mane in that area should be trimmed, then push the head collar to the back and remove the mane from in front, up to the back of the forelock. Then push the head collar right back behind the cut area and tidy up by running the scissors or clippers against a comb over the trimmed area.

In the case of advanced skin infections, the mane should be hogged in order to assist in the treatment.

The Shaven Look

Sometimes it is necessary to clip out the mane completely– this is also called hogging. This is not only for certain types of horses such as cobs, but can also be called for on medical grounds. This is especially the case for horses suffering from sweet itch, that need to be treated with creams or lotions along the crest. A scabby and infected crest can't be treated if a thick mane, tangled by constant rubbing, is covering the site of the infection. In such cases hogging can help enormously, making effective treatment pos-sible. This decision should be made in consultation with your vet, since hogging also removes an important protective weapon against insects and may, without the correct treatment, actually worsen the condition.

Rubbed or spiky manes can be hogged and should as a result grow back more evenly. Several points, however, must be noted:

• Afterwards the horse will have no reliable in-built protection from the weather and may not be able to be kept in the same way as before.

• Without a protective mane, insects are able to do their worst.

Whoever is responsible for the care of the horse must therefore ensure that something takes the place of this natural weather and fly protection, ideally by providing suitable shelter and regularly applying insect repellents, or using one of the many specialist fly rugs or sheets that often include a hood.

Hogging

Clippers are noisy objects and because of their vibration will feel strange as well. If your horse can watch a stable mate being clipped, or if it is able to be fed its hard feed from a wide-mouthed bucket during clipping, then it is more likely to settle faster and stand up during clipping. If this doesn't work then there is no choice but to use hand clippers. These take longer and the result doesn't look as even, but they are far less dangerous for horse and owner.

Very dense or tangled manes should first be cut short with scissors or hand clippers and then, starting from the withers, the clippers should be run flat up the length of the

Roddy is given his feed during clipping – he thinks clipping's great!

Shortly after hogging the mane will start to grow back.

crest. Most horses don't find this quite as bad and with luck it will have become used to the noise before things get critical at the poll.

With the head collar pushed well forward, clip up to the poll, then stop and put the clippers down. Move the head collar back and clip the rest from front to back. Then go over it again without breaking off in order to get as even a look as possible. In the case of sweet itch, if it is healed then the mane should grow back evenly on the bald patches too, but it will grow back as a standing mane. By the following summer the mane should be long enough to offer good protection from flies. But remember that in the first winter after hogging, your horse will be missing the insulating warmth of its mane!

Thanks to plaiting, good-looking horses and ponies look even better.

Plaited Up for Competition

As the final touch for many occasions – competitions, breed shows or events, manes and tails are dressed accordingly; traditionally this means the mane at least will be plaited. The more plaits, the better the overall picture, while making the most of a horse's top line.

If the mane is out of the way, the top of the whip won't get tangled up, and even horses with sparse manes can look elegant and well turned out. If you think plaiting is a waste of time, remember that a well turned out horse is also a reflection of its owner, and of the worth he or she places in the horse.

Plaiting – Step by step

To get the best results, the mane should first be pulled evenly to a length of at least a hand's breadth. Have a wet sponge, a mane comb and sufficient plaiting bands handy, as well as a stool in the case of larger horses. Dampen the forelock and mane before starting, and carefully comb so that the entire mane lies on one side and there is a clear parting between the forelock and the mane. The steps to follow are shown below.

1. Take a section of mane and plait firmly to the end, fastening it with a rubber band.

2. The end of the plait should be folded up underneath (i.e. in half) and the rubber band wound round once, then the doubled plait should be folded back underneath again and the rubber band wound round once more, or use a second rubber band if necessary, making sure it is secured tightly. With short manes you may only need to fold up once.

3. If you use black bands with black manes, the resulting bunches with look uniformly dark, although some people prefer to use contrasting bands. It is also possible to use white bands when using plaiting tape wound around each plait.

The number of plaits depends on the enthusiasm of the plaiter and the thicknes of the mane, although it is usually advantageous to do more rather than less. Not only does this look better, but also the plaits are more likely to stay in when they are put under the stress of the horse starting to work in an outline.

4. For uncut longer or natural manes you can also plait up the whole mane in long plaits and then on the day of the show undo them for a wavy look.

Looks good and is simple to do: the Spanish plait.

A Touch of Elegance and Colour

A particularly attractive look is a thick plait that runs down the length of the crest; this is seen primarily on Spanish horses. It's not only Andalusians that this method is used on though; this is seen in other breeds with sufficiently thick and long manes such as Friesians and heavy horses. The mane is kept out of the way of both horse and rider, the top line is enhanced and it does look great. If desired, a wide ribbon or cord can be plaited in, for example in the national colours of the breed's country of origin.

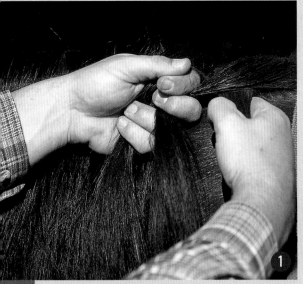 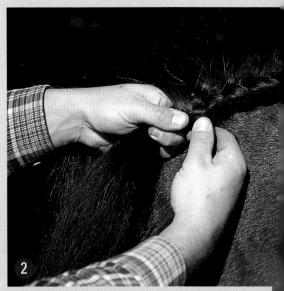

1. Beginning behind the poll, take up a thick strand and divide it into three. This is how you plait a mane lying to the right: after first putting the right and then left section over the middle one (as in a normal plait), the following steps are repeated over and over.

2. Put the right section over the middle one, add in some more of the remaining mane to the left section and put this over the middle one. Put the right section over the new middle one, and so on.

3. The plait is done exactly as with a normal plait, except that the section on the wither side of the plait is added to each tim round with mane. This helps to keep the plait lying close to the crest while growing down the neck.

Ribbon or wool can be plaited into one or more sections, and can look particularly attractive.

If the mane lies to the left, then do exactly the opposite, adding the new strands from the mane to the right section of the plait. When reaching the withers the rest of the mane is plaited out and secured with the rubber band. If you wish, ribbon or cord can be plaited in at the same time by adding it in at the start, using a hidden knot to keep it in place and then incorporating it into one or more of the three sections. Doing this makes sparse manes look thicker; and thinner necks can benefit from a coloured plait.

Mane designs

The thick and heavy manes of many ponies often don't allow themselves to be plaited easily. For special occasions you can use ribbons or coloured tape to make patterns with the mane. First, wash and comb out the mane.

Instead of plaiting bands, use colourful hair bands or ribbon bows.

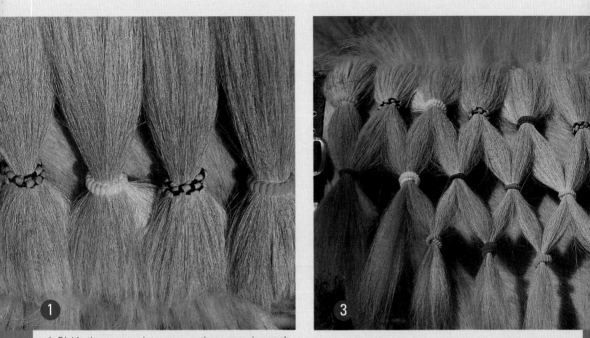

1. Divide the mane up into even sections, securing each one about 10 cm down from the crest with a plaiting band or similar.

3. Repeat step 2 as often as required until the whole mane is tied in its pattern

2. Next, each strand should be divided in two just below the plaiting band. Each half is then paired up with its neighbour to right or left, and the new strand should be secured, again 10 cm below the first row of bands.

Good From the Rear

Ponies and heavy horses with thick tails look particularly good with plaited tails. While with mane plaiting the entire length of the hair is grasped, with the tails usually only three sections are used to form the plait, which lies on top of the tail; this means the entire length of the tail is not actually plaited. Incidentally, horses that tend to kick out behind are usually marked in public with a red ribbon in their tail

This warning sign means: Keep your distance!

First wash and comb the tail, dampening it again before starting to plait.

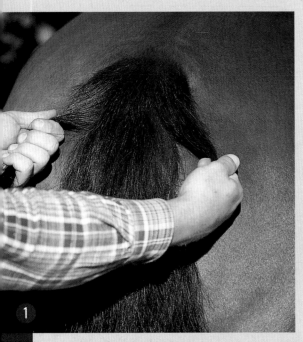

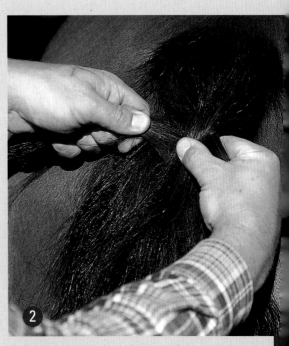

1. At the top of the tail, sort out three sections: one in the middle and one on either side.

2. After the first plait (once from the left, once from the right), add in strands from either left or right before plaiting over again until the end of the dock is reached. Continue to plait down as normal without adding in, and secure with a rubber band, folded up once and tied again.

3. The plait needs to be kept tight, otherwise it won't lie flat and will quickly undo.

4. The tail can be plaited to the bottom if wished, or secured half way up

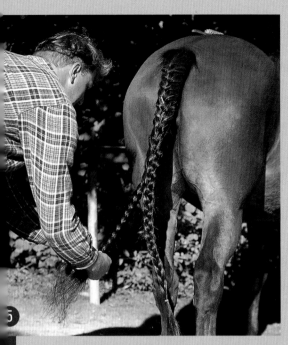

5. Professional's tip: plait the tail into two plaits from the dock down. Leave it in overnight and take out the next day.

6. The permed look may stay in for only a couple of hours, but it's worth it, isn't it?

7. The washed or plaited tail should be protected until the start of competition with either a tail wrap…

8. … or a tail bandage so that it doesn't get dirty or start to unravel.

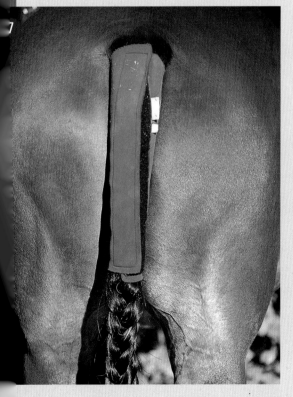

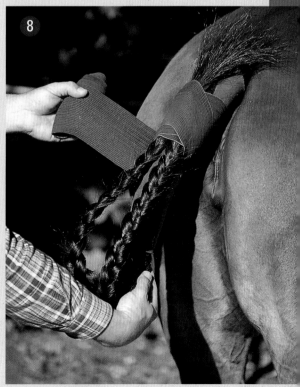

Dotting the I's

When stepping out in public; you and your horse should fulfil at least the following criteria:

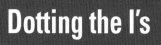

Tips

• Your horse should be correctly shod, or if unshod, the hoofs should be tidy and trimmed.
• Mane and tail should be freshly washed and combed.
• The horse should be washed, or at least well groomed. White markings should be white, not yellow.
• Eyes and nostrils should be clean.
•All tack should of course be cleaned and checked before the event.
• The feeding regime of your horse should also have been considered.

When stepping out in public, you and your horse should present a tidy picture.

Finishing touches

With a few final touches; your horse can look even better.

Using coat shine makes it easier to comb out manes. Spray onto mane and tail, let it dry and then comb out carefully.

The hair growing inside the ears fulfil an important role and should not be shaved. It doesn't harm the horse, however, if the protruding hairs are trimmed back evenly. To do this, grasp the ear and squeeze the edges gently together. With scissors, trim back the protruding hairs to the edge. In the case of strong, nervous or ticklish horses; leave this to someone more experienced!

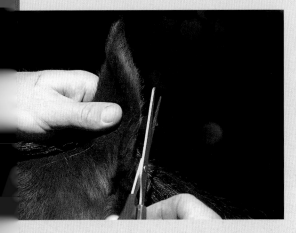

A little baby oil around the eyes and nostrils can enhance a horse's expression. Put several drops on your hands, rub them together and then stroke around the eyes and nostrils. This is; however; not to everyone's taste.

For safety:
- *Always wear sturdy or safety footwear.*
- *Tie up horses to a secured ring or place, preferably at your horse's jaw height.*
- *Ensure that there is firm footing.*
- *Clear away any dangerous machinery or tools, such as hayforks.*
- *Take care that the horse can't stand on the clipper cable.*
- *Use scissors with rounded ends, and always maintain body contact with your horse through your hand.*
- *Never stand directly behind your horse and when dealing with the tail, stand to one side.*
- *Never become impatient, or work to too tight a schedule.*

Safety Tips

In caring for horses, you should always act with safety in mind – your own, your horse's and that of anyone else around. It is better to do without clipping or trimming around sensitive parts of the horse than to upset or unsettle him. Even with a calm or sensible horse, you should always be prepared for something to upset him – all horses are by their nature flight animals, and tend towards sudden reactions when startled.